PABLITA VELARDE

PABLITA VELARDE

By Mary Carroll Nelson

DILLON PRESS

MINNEAPOLIS, MINNESOTA

© 1971 by Dillon Press, Inc. All rights reserved

Dillon Press, Inc.
Minneapolis, Minnesota 55401

Standard Book Number: 87518-037-X
Library of Congress Catalog Card Number: 77-140992

Printed in the United States of America

ON THE COVER:
Pablita Velarde working on an earth painting.

PABLITA VELARDE

Pablita Velarde Hardin is a famous Tewa Indian artist, born in Santa Clara Pueblo, New Mexico, on September 19, 1918. Pablita Velarde has helped revive and reinterpret traditional Indian art forms — preserving them for the pleasure of people today and for future generations. She also wrote and illustrated *Old Father, the Story Teller,* a book of Tewa legends.

Pablita's story tells of the conflict between her Indian heritage and her life in the Anglo world.

Contents

CHAPTER I

Golden Dawn is Born

September is a golden month in northern New Mexico. The cottonwoods turn a beautiful, glowing yellow. The sun shines day in and day out, warming the earth at harvest time. Melons, peaches, apples, corn, beans, and squashes ripen, and the Indians gather food to store for the winter.

In the pueblo of Santa Clara, fall was just beginning and the nights were growing chilly. Many families had returned from the mountains where they spent the summer. Herman Velarde, the farmer and trapper, his wife, Marianita, and their two little girls, Standing Cloud and Flower were waiting for the birth of another baby.

Grandmother Velarde was there to help Marianita with the birth. Marianita's own mother had died, so Herman's mother, Qualupita, had to help. Qualupita was a medicine woman. She was the doctor if the Indians were sick, and she delivered the babies.

At about daylight, a little girl was born.

The Pueblo Indians believe that the spirit of a newborn baby does not come to earth at the same time the baby does. For four days the baby has no name while the family waits for its spirit to come. Many Pueblo babies died soon after birth. It was this sad fact that probably caused the Indians to believe the spirit of the newborn takes a few days to arrive; sometimes it does not arrive at all. The spirit of a person is thought of as the life within him.

After four days, Qualupita came to perform the naming ceremony for the new baby. The many aunts came, too. Qualupita placed hot coals and two pieces of pine bark in a pottery bowl. She carried the bowl outdoors and offered it in her outstretched hands to the six directions. She held it up, and then down, and then to the north, south, east, and west. This offering is made to ask that the child's life will have warmth, and brighten the lives of others. Next, she took the little baby girl and offered her to the six directions. Qualupita sprinkled corn meal by the doorway while she prayed for a good life, a worthy life, and a healthy life for the baby. As she made the offering, she said, "I name you Tse Tsan."

Inside the adobe house, Qualupita offered medicine water to all the people who were there. Each person took a turn and gave another name to the newborn child. Usually these names are forgotten, although sometimes a funny one might become a nickname for a child. But the honor of really naming the baby goes to the grandmother. If the mother's mother is alive, she is the grandmother who does this—but if not, the father's mother does it. Qualupita, the medicine woman, chose a beautiful name. Tse Tsan means "Golden Dawn" in English. Little did the family know that this tiny baby girl would someday be one of the most famous Indian artists in the world.

It is the Indian custom to place a baby on a cradle board, instead of using a playpen. The child is wrapped in a soft blanket or quilt, and then is tied with leather laces onto a board. The board is slung between two leather loops hanging from the vigas. The vigas are the wooden beams that cross the ceiling. As the older children or the parents pass by the cradle board, they swing it gently. The baby can watch everything that is going on, and the swinging keeps it happy and puts it to sleep. Babies do not stay on the cradle board all day, only when the mother is busy. At other times, she wraps her baby in a shawl and hangs it around her shoulder, either in front, or in the back.

Golden Dawn had the same babyhood as any other infant in Santa Clara. As she grew a bit older, she learned to toddle around holding onto the hands of her older sisters. The tiny, brown-eyed child learned to walk on the dried mud floors of her adobe house. The house had two rooms. One room was the living area where the family slept. The other was the kitchen and eating room. Like all the other houses in Santa Clara, the Velarde home had a fireplace with a chimney. Much of the cooking was done indoors on a wood stove. An Indian baby learns to eat the same food as the family as soon as possible. Sometimes the baby is given things to suck on, like sugar cane or the sweet stalks of young corn. When Marianita sprinkled the floor with water just before she swept it, Golden Dawn loved the smell of the wet mud; sometimes she would scoop up a little in her hands and eat that, too.

As she grew a bit, Golden Dawn began to eat Indian foods such as sakaweh, which is the Tewa name for cornmeal mush. Sakaweh and fry bread are two foods the Velardes had often. Fry bread is a tortilla that is dropped into hot grease, making it puff up like a doughnut. The family spread jam or, sometimes, molasses on the fry bread.

The Indians baked fat, golden loaves of bread in the horno — the round little structure that looks like a bee hive, but is really an outdoor oven. Each home has a horno in the yard; if possible, it is placed under a tree for shade. Hornos are not all exactly alike; some are smaller, and some are larger. The Indian women use long wooden paddles to reach into the oven to pull out the bread when it is done. Golden Dawn grew up smelling the bread baking, piñon pine logs burning in the fireplace, and hot chili bubbling in the pot on the stove.

When Herman Velarde shot a deer, the family could not freeze the meat to save it, because they had no freezer. So they dried what was not eaten. In summer, there are many greens growing on the reservation, such as wild spinach, wide-leafed pig weed, bee weed, and sometimes, tender wild asparagus. These were delicacies. Rabbits and turkeys were found more often on the reservation. They were cooked on a large grill in the outdoor fireplace.

The smells of good food and the close feelings of being in a family were a happy part of Golden Dawn's childhood, but they were mixed with bad times, too. None of the Santa Clara Indians were well-off during the 1920s when she was growing up. Sometimes food was very scarce. Times were especially bad during those years when there was hardly any rain and crops failed to grow. The Indian people live very close to the earth; they depend on themselves to grow and to gather most of what they need. When nature is cruel, sending little water, the people suffer. Golden Dawn learned about suffering early in her life.

When Golden Dawn was about three, the family was sad-

A Santa Clara horno.

dened by the death of her mother, Marianita. Marianita had tuberculosis, a dread disease in the pueblo. At that time, 1921, tuberculosis was not easily cured. Many Indians caught it. Tuberculosis is an infection of the lungs. As the infection grows worse, the disease weakens a person until he has lost all strength and can no longer breathe. Today we have medicines that cure tuberculosis patients, but Marianita did not get any help for her illness. She, like many other Indians, died at a young age from this killing disease. A public health doctor told Herman the name of Marianita's disease, and explained the value of sunshine and fresh air for the family. The Indian people know a great many things about curing sickness and making medicines. They do not have the same ideas about illness that doctors in hospitals have. In the Indian faith, illness is believed to come from evil spirits. Because he believed that illness can be passed from one person to another, Herman made the family sleep outdoors. Except when it rained, they all spent most of their time outside. Even the baby, Little Turquoise Ray or Jane, slept under the trees. Little Turquoise Ray was just a few months old when Marianita died. Herman's actions may seem strange, but they were probably the wisest ones to take. He kept his girls out of the house, a source of tuberculosis germs. None of the rest of the family caught the disease.

Herman Velarde had not seen the end of trouble. Not long after losing their mother, Golden Dawn and Little Turquoise Ray were struck by a mysterious illness that took away their eyesight. Golden Dawn's eyes became so infected that she grew blind. Her blindness, and that of her little sister, lasted for many months. Herman Velarde was not a medicine man, but he was one of the few people in the pueblo of Santa Clara who knew ways to make medicines from the plants that grow on the reservation. Herman knew about some of the old medicines from his mother, Qualupita. He also tried out many new ones, experimenting on himself by drinking the medicines he made. Herman was searching for a cure for his daughters' illness. After nearly two years, both children regained their sight, although Golden Dawn's left eye was permanently weak. Her sister's eyes were also affected; they were left lighter in color than they had been before. No one in the family knows what type of infection attacked the children, or what medicine cured them.

The Velardes' house was at the edge of the pueblo, with its own yard and garden. It was an adobe house made from clay bricks and covered with the rose-pink sandy mud of the region. The mud dries to a surface that is smooth, like on a piece of pottery. Buildings, roads, and hills all share the rosy color of the earth in the region of Santa Clara. All around the outskirts of the pueblo, the mountains add their backdrop of beauty to the landscape. The mountains seem to be made of straight, strong lines. The layers of earth and rocks that formed the mountains still can be seen in the edges, which look like steps. The same shape of flat, long rectangles put together like steps is seen in the pueblo buildings. Some of them are more than one story high. Many of them touch each other, so that they form a long block of houses. Leaning against the building are wooden ladders made from rough tree trunks that are thin but strong. The Indians use the ladders to get up on the roof, or to get into second story doorways. Here and there in the pueblo are tall cottonwood trees that give some shade to the village. In the center of the pueblo is a plaza, or open square, with buildings clustered around it.

Two places in the pueblo were especially important to little Golden Dawn. One was the plaza where she could watch the Indian dances at fiesta time. The fiesta is a holiday time for celebrating. Part of the celebration in the pueblo is the traditional dance. Each dance has a name and particular type of costume. Some of the dances the child saw in the plaza are the deer dance, buffalo dance, rain dance, eagle dance, corn dance, and belt dance. Many people dance together at the Indian fiestas; sometimes the children join in the dancing. Often the men dance, and the women and children just watch. The costumes for the dances are beautiful, but sometimes they can also be frightening. Golden Dawn, like the other children at Santa Clara, was afraid of the Kachina figure. The Kachina wore a huge headdress, making him seem extremely tall. The little girl looked at the Kachina and thought he was magic; with his face hidden behind the masked headdress, and his arms covered by eagle feathers, he seemed like a magic bird. The scenes of her pueblo plaza made a deep impression in Golden Dawn's mind.

The other place in the pueblo that was important to Golden Dawn was the ancient church. In Santa Clara there is an old mission church of adobe with a wooden beamed ceiling. Golden Dawn went to mass with her family when the priest came, about once a month, by horse and buggy. He also came at Easter and Christmas. On St. Claire's feast day, August twelfth, the pueblo had a fiesta with a mass and dances. The dances of her people were the ancient Indian religious custom; the mass was the ancient Christian religious custom. Golden Dawn learned both customs as a child.

Earth painting: Kachina and mud head clowns.

CHAPTER II

School Days, Summer Days

Herman Velarde was a modern Indian. He wanted his children to be educated. There was a day school at Santa Clara where Legoria (Standing Cloud) and Rosita (Flower) had gone for a year. Herman could have sent all of his daughters there, but it would not have solved his problem. He could not farm and trap for furs without a wife to care for his girls. What he needed was a boarding school that could provide care, day and night, for his children.

One day in 1924, when Golden Dawn was almost six, and her sisters were seven and twelve, Herman bundled them into his wagon and drove them thirty miles to Santa Fe. Only Jane (Little Turquoise Ray) remained behind, still too tiny to go to school. Herman enrolled the three older children in the St. Catherine's Indian School, run by the Catholic missionary Sisters of the Blessed Sacrament. It was a large school with big buildings for the children to live in; one dormitory was for the boys and there was another for the girls. Golden Dawn was awed by the big buildings, which were the largest ones she had ever seen. All around her were children, and there were also nuns, in their long, black dresses and starched white headdresses. The child had not learned English before her trip to school, so Golden Dawn

could not understand a word. Her sisters, Legoria and Rosita, had picked up some English in the day school. They got along quite well. Golden Dawn followed them about, doing what they did, listening to the strange sounds. She missed the pueblo, her father Herman, her little sister Jane, and Qualupita. Here at school, she could not smell the warm bread baking in the horno. Here, she could not play with the little squirrels that came up to the door of her adobe at Santa Clara. Here, she could not curl up at her father's feet after the long day, or hear him tell stories of the ancient people, her people, in the days long ago. Golden Dawn was lonely. As it grew dark, the children went into the dormitory to get ready for bed. The boys went into their own building, and the girls went into theirs, up the stairs to the long sleeping rooms. Each girl had her own cot, and a few clothes put away in the cupboard. Neither Golden Dawn nor her sisters had much of their own. Their father had not brought much with them. Golden Dawn huddled down in the strange bed, her mind filled with the words of her own Tewa language. She heard the other girls speaking to each other in English. Not all of the girls were from the pueblos. Some of them were Navajos from reservations quite far away. Some were from other pueblos, such as San Ildefonso, San Domingo, Laguna, and Zuni. All of the girls were speaking English. Golden Dawn listened to the sounds of their voices, but she could not understand them.

The next day, Golden Dawn began to go to school. She was too young for the first grade and was put into a class like kindergarten to help children get ready for first grade. The tall lady in the black dress said to her, "Hello, Pablita." Golden Dawn did not know the sounds or what they meant, but she watched, and she kept listening. Over and over, people said to her, "Hello, Pablita." No one said her Tewa name, "Tse Tsan." It was not long before Golden Dawn got used to her new name, Pablita Velarde. This name, her Christian name, is Spanish. It means the same as **Pauline**, or the girl's name for Paul. It is a saint's name.

During the first year Pablita Velarde spent in school, she began to understand the words that were spoken so quickly by everyone else. She began to speak English.

The nuns who ran the school were very fair. They treated the children alike and did not have favorites. Sister Frances slept behind a curtain in one corner of the long dormitory bedroom; she was there to comfort anyone who needed her during the night. Sister Ann, an elderly nun, saw to it that the children washed and dressed. She was like an older mother. The sisters were poor, depending on charity for the food they needed to feed the Indian children. The diet at school was not too different from the pueblo. At breakfast, there might be oatmeal with weak coffee; at noon, bread and gravy; and for supper, beans with an apple. It was simple, but nourishing food.

During the day, Pablita played with any group that was having fun. She liked people and was a happy child, playing hopscotch and jacks. Ever since her mother died, Pablita and her sisters had been outside most of the time. Pablita enjoyed playing outside more than she liked to be in the classroom.

Pablita and her sisters stayed throughout the winter at St. Catherine's. They did not go home for any vacations, even though the family was only thirty miles away. Sometimes they wrote letters to their father, and Herman would answer them. About twice a year, he went into Santa Fe to see his children, staying only a few minutes. Herman gave the girls a little money, maybe as much as fifty cents, and went away again — leaving the children behind. Pablita and her sisters spent the months from September to June at St. Catherine's.

In the summer, Pablita lived a very different life. Herman would come for the girls and take them home to Santa Clara. Herman had no sons, so his daughters learned to do things to help him on the farm. They wore blue jeans with tattered shirts and ran barefoot. All of them were excellent riders and spent much of the summer on horseback. They knew how to lead cattle out of the pen in the morning, and back in again at night. After the family moved up into the mountain on the Santa Clara reservation for the summer months, the girls made a daily trip riding down the mountainside carrying water kegs on their horses. At the bottom they filled the kegs at the Santa Clara creek, and then rode the mile or so up to the flat mountain top where Herman was dry farming. He was raising corn, squash, beans, and peas, trusting there would be enough rain to water his crops. The water the girls hauled was for drinking and cooking. Legoria, the oldest girl, did the cooking for the family. In the mountains they lived in a log cabin, but spent most of their time outside. Legoria did the cooking outdoors, over a fire.

Pablita's family life during her years in St. Catherine's was a changing one. For two years, her father was married to a fine woman named Clara Naranjo. She was a very neat person and watched carefully to see that the children washed before eating and followed up-to-date hygiene. After Herman and Clara had been married about two years, Clara died while giving birth to a son. Somehow, with the help of his mother and sisters, Herman kept the small baby alive for about three months. Then it, too, died.

Once again Herman Velarde was a widower. Once again the Velarde children had lost a mother, although they had hardly known her. Herman continued to provide for his girls as well as he could. When he needed help, he turned to Qualupita.

When they were in the pueblo, the Velarde sisters often stayed with their grandmother, the medicine woman. Qualupita lived in the plaza, in a house attached to many others. After the work of the day was over, the girls stayed down by the plaza, and ate with Qualupita. They were as at home with her as they were in their own little house on the outskirts of the pueblo. Pablita learned many customs and skills from her grandmother.

Every so often an old peddler from Abiquiu, a village in the northern country known as "Ghost Ranch," came down to the pueblo with large clumps of gypsum rock. Qualupita roasted the gypsum in the outdoor oven. Then she crushed it into a powder. She mixed a big tub of whitewash and added the gypsum powder. This mixture was used to paint the walls of the houses. Little decoration is used on the walls of the Santa Clara houses, but the Indians do use paint to decorate the borders of the doors, windows, and fireplaces. They use flat designs, with stripes and stepped patterns that are symbols for the mountains and for rain. In the Kiva, the sacred building used for important meetings in the pueblo, there are more elaborate wall paintings. Pablita had seen them there. Pablita saw her relatives painting patterns on their walls, too, during her childhood years.

All of Pablita's aunts and also Qualupita were good potters. The Velarde girls often watched them form the clay into pots and later decorate them. The women let the children try to make their own pots, and then to decorate them. The Santa Clara pueblo is known for its black pottery, a distinctive, shiny style. By watching their elders at work, the children learned how to make pottery in the Santa Clara designs. It is in this fashion that Indians teach their children the ways of their people.

The Velarde girls enjoyed their life in the pueblo in those days. Every day they listened to the sounds of the Denver and Rio Grande train tooting its whistle as it passed the pueblo. People at Santa Clara timed their days by the train whistle of the "Chili Line," so-called because the valley is known for growing chili peppers. At noon, when the train blew its whistle, everyone stopped for lunch. In the late afternoon, the workwagon blew a toot on its way home, so everyone in Santa Clara knew it was the end of the workday. There were no shops in Santa Clara, so the Indians did their shopping in Española, a small town about two miles from the pueblo. They usually followed the railroad tracks and walked into town. But occasionally, if they had some money, they would hail the engineer on the train and he would stop to pick them up. He took them into Española for one nickel, and would take them home again for another. Pablita looked forward to the train rides; nickels were hard to come by during her childhood, so her trips by train were not frequent. The train tracks were taken up during World War II. The friendly sound of the tooting whistle is now just a memory.

Above Santa Clara there are remains of ancient cliff

*Pablita and painting
that shows Puye pictographs.*

dwellings, the Puye Ruins. The ruins are some miles from the pueblo, but still on the reservation. About five hundred years ago, there were two thousand rooms in the main house of the cliff dwellings. Puye is known as the "Pueblo of the Clouds." The ancestors of the Santa Clara people once lived on the plateau, farming quietly, and living a settled life. Repeated raids by the Navajo tribe threatened their peace just at the time of a long drought. At first, the Cliff Dwellers tried to protect themselves by burrowing into the caves in the mountains, but bringing up water from the valley was no longer safe. The Cliff Dwellers finally moved to the valley and established their present pueblo.

Playing in these ruins was a favorite summer pastime for Pablita and her sisters. When they were not working around the farm, they went on treasure hunts in the ruins. Climbing about on the steep cliff of reddish-gold rock, they poked into the caves that were behind the cliff houses. They hunted for arrowheads and pieces of pottery. Here and there, in the remains of the ancient houses, the children found pieces of flat rock that had pictures on them. When Pablita found one of these rock pictures she would pretend that she was an ancient one and then try to imagine what the life of her ancestors might have been. These pictures with their flat, simple designs stayed in her mind. Years later, she still remembered clearly the way she had felt as a child playing on the Puye Mesa, and her wonder at finding the rock pictures.

The dark blindness Pablita had known early in her childhood left her with a lifelong delight in seeing. She studies everything she sees, so small details stay in her mind almost as though they were photographed. While climbing among the Puye Ruins with her sisters or watching her elders at their daily tasks, the young Pablita began to collect mental pictures of scenes from her pueblo life.

On summer nights, the family gathered around the fire outdoors after supper. Herman Velarde entertained his children with stories. He knew the legends of his people by heart. In winter, he told tales in his adobe house in the valley. Sometimes he told his stories in the plaza around a large bonfire, sharing them with many children besides his own, and the adults as well. Herman was a respected man in the pueblo, filling the role of storyteller. Long after dark the stories might continue, with the children eagerly listening. Indians do not put their children to bed early or cut them off from hearing the talk of their elders. Pablita heard Herman's stories many times and in this way learned the traditional beliefs of her people. Most of Herman's tales were religious ones, or myths.

One of Pablita's favorite stories was about the beginnings of the pueblo people on the earth. In this story, the people come up from their first home underground and are led to a safe home by Spider Woman. The stars, the sun, and the moon are all part of the story. This is the pueblo creation myth that Herman often told. Herman's tales stayed in Pablita's mind, too, filling her imagination with scenes from the life of the ancient ones.

CHAPTER III

Pigment and Praise

St. Catherine's was an elementary school. After sixth grade, Pablita had to move across the city of Santa Fe to the United States Indian School, which was run by the Bureau of Indian Affairs (BIA). She entered the eighth grade, the same grade her sister Rosita was in, skipping the seventh grade altogether. For her future, 1932 was a lucky year to go to the Indian School; it was the same year that a fine teacher named Dorothy Dunn came from Chicago to teach there.

At the Indian School, Dorothy Dunn introduced Pablita to a new world — a world of paint, designs, lines, and pictures. Young boys and girls from many tribes attended this big school on the south edge of Santa Fe. Miss Dunn encouraged them to learn their own tribal symbols, and to share them with one another. In this way, the Indian artists began to create a style of painting that was unlike the art of any other group. It was their own cultural tradition that they were learning, not the Anglo or white man's culture. Almost all by herself, Dorothy Dunn taught a large group of Indians to express their own history in their own art. Many of the most famous Indian artists were her pupils; many were classmates of Pablita. Dorothy Dunn established the first

Indian art studio in any school in the entire United States.

Miss Dunn believed in the value of the Indian's culture. It was her hope that the studio pupils would think about their life at home and then make pictures in their own way to show the Indian way of living. Although she wanted the Indian pupils to develop their own art styles, she taught them basic facts about colors, about the way a brush behaves, and about drawing. The students experimented with ancient methods of grinding raw clays and stones to make their own pigments; this was training that Pablita put to good use later in her life.

Rather than asking her students to draw an action figure from a model, she asked them to try to express the action from memory. For Pablita, this system worked very well.

Pablita had grown used to memorizing what she saw. As she thought back over her childhood, certain memories stood out. She especially remembered the jobs women did in the pueblo. Much of her early art centered around the women of Santa Clara at their daily work.

When Pablita first began to paint, she did a drawing of Santa Clara women molding brown clay into large jars, called "ollas." She had seen such an activity many times in her life. It was familiar subjects like this that Dorothy Dunn had hoped her students would draw or paint. At first, Pablita sketched a number of trial drawings. The she did a drawing in charcoal and colored it in with chalk. After she had a picture she liked, she did a careful pencil drawing on watercolor paper, and then painted it in with tempera paint. Tempera paint is thicker than watercolor. Pablita finished her painting by adding outlines on top of these painted areas. The shapes of the women and jars were flat. She did

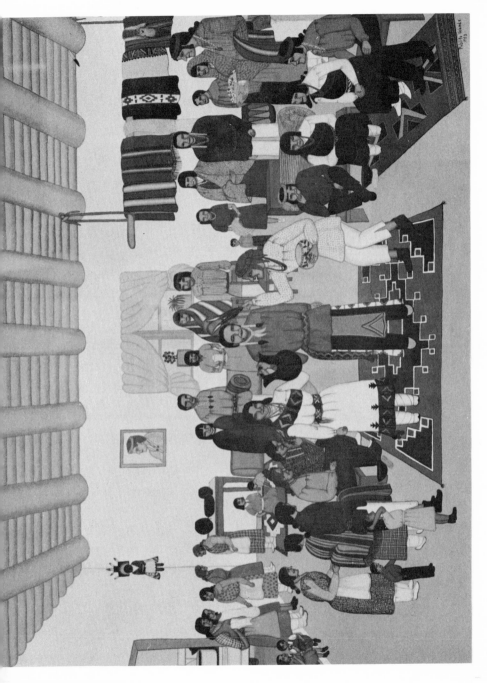

Casein water color of Pueblo Indian wedding.

not try to make them look round. The colors of her first painting were bright, and the whole picture looked simple and honest.

Dorothy Dunn liked Pablita's work, but more important, Pablita had liked doing it. Her mind was filled with other ideas for pictures, and she felt sure she could draw other subjects if she tried. During her first year in Miss Dunn's class, Pablita learned to paint very well. She no longer drew the designs so many times; instead, she drew right onto the piece of paper for the final picture. She worked very hard.

Pablita clearly remembered the excitement of ceremonials. The costumes, with all their decorations, became one of her favorite subjects. She learned to draw so well that in one picture she could put a whole scene of the plaza with dancers doing the steps and making the hand gestures, surrounded by the buildings and spectators. She had vivid memories of animals. The horses she rode down the mountain for water were now exciting subjects for paintings. The deer that came up to the adobe door at Santa Clara, the road runners which are the New Mexico state bird, and many other animals, filled her pictures with life.

After she became an artist, Pablita found she could think about her pueblo life almost as though it were a movie. She could see the scenes of her childhood, full of details and action. She, herself, was like a spectator. The more she painted about her pueblo, the more she was separated from it. Her art was not done for Indians to see. It was meant to be seen by other people at exhibitions, or in homes, perhaps. Pablita's art was meant to tell about the Indians to someone else. To paint this way, Pablita had to think differently from most Indians who are not artists, and from non-Indians who did not grow up as she did. Even as a teenager, Pablita felt different from other people, caught somewhere between the Indian world and the non-Indian one.

At the end of the first year, with much excitement, the Indian School Studio prepared to put on an all-Indian art show. Part of it was going to be shown at the Museum of New Mexico, and part of it was going to be hung at the Indian School itself. Many people were going to come to it. Pablita and her older sister, Rosita, did a number of paintings showing their own pueblo and the life of the women there, all from memory. Some of Pablita's paintings were titled, "Women Baking Bread," "Women Husking Corn," and "Women with Ollas."

In Santa Fe, there was an artist named Olive Rush. Miss Rush came to see the show of the work by Miss Dunn's pupils. She liked it, and she knew a way to get many others to see it. Olive Rush was a mural painter, which means she painted pictures on walls. She had been asked to prepare some murals on masonite panels that were to be shown in Chicago at a very important fair called the "Century of Progress." She asked Miss Dunn if some of the Indian pupils would like to help. Pablita was one of the three pupils selected to work with Miss Rush. An oil painting on masonite of a Santa Clara girl by Pablita was sent to the "Century of Progress" exhibit in 1933. Many people saw the work of this talented, young Indian girl — a girl barely finished with the eighth grade.

In 1933, the Federal Government began paying for art projects in Santa Fe. Some of the Indian students were invited to work on murals. Pablita Velarde signed up to do a mural in oils on masonite. Her painting was of pueblo life in Santa Clara. She also did a number of small watercolors about her pueblo. These paintings were shown to the public in both New Mexico and Washington, D. C.

Like the rest of Miss Dunn's pupils, Pablita did not copy from another artist. Instead she developed her own style. She was the only girl who took all of the art classes at the studio. After only one year of classes, Pablita had been chosen to do three special art projects. She was a humble girl, and a shy one, but she knew that painting was something she could do well. Each time she was selected to paint a picture, she had to study, sketch, and plan her work. She became a better and better artist, able to use more materials. At the pueblo, the job of painting is not considered a woman's work, but a man's. By working as an artist, Pablita was behaving in a way that was different from other pueblo girls. She was considered a rebel, someone who does not act like everyone else.

The longer Pablita was in school, the more unusual she became. In those days, not too many Indians, especially Indian girls, stayed in school through high school. Most of them were dropouts. Pablita stayed on. Herman allowed her to stay. At that time, Pablita was not interested in marrying. If she had been, however, no one would have kept her from leaving school to marry.

During Pablita's first year at the Indian School, her father married once again. This time his wife was a very young woman, not too much older than Legoria. Her name was Rose. Herman and Rose had a family of one son and two daughters. Pablita, Rosita, and Jane did not feel close to their father's new family. Legoria had also gotten married. She was only a young teenager, not much more than fifteen years old when she married. Her husband, Pasqual, was somewhat older, nearly twenty. He became a big brother to Legoria's sisters. When Pablita, Rosita, and Jane came home to the pueblo, it was to Legoria's new home, not to Herman's. Pasqual looked after them, listened to them, and sheltered them. Pablita did not see as much of Herman, nor have many conversations with him for several years.

However, Herman was still her father, and it was up to him to make decisions for Pablita's future. He was afraid Pablita could not earn any money if all she ever did was paint. He talked to his daughter about learning to type so that she could get a good secretarial job when she graduated. The Indian School did not offer business classes at that time, so it was decided that Pablita would stop going to school at Santa Fe and transfer to Española High School. Herman was not trying to be mean to Pablita. He knew how hard it was to get work, and he was thinking of her best interests.

Pablita moved home. It was hard for her to get used to being at home all the time. She had lived in boarding schools for more than ten years. When she went home, Rose and Herman were like strangers to her. Their three small children did not seem like a brother and sisters to Pablita. The house was crowded with her in it. Every day Pablita walked along the railroad tracks to the high school, and back again in the afternoon. She missed her work with Miss Dunn and the other pupils in Santa Fe. After eighteen months, she had taken all the business courses offered by Española High School. She transferred back to the Santa Fe Indian School to be with her old classmates for half a year more. In 1936, Pablita graduated from the United States Indian School of

Santa Fe. She was the first of her family to get all the way through high school. Herman had left school in the eighth grade. Legoria had left to marry, and so did Rosita. Only Pablita got her diploma. It was time for her to earn her own living.

CHAPTER IV

Free and Independent

Pablita was eighteen years old. It was early summer in 1936, a time when there were few jobs for anyone and even fewer for Indians. She went home to wait until school started in the fall.

In September, Pablita was employed at the day school in Santa Clara as a teaching assistant. Her job was to teach arts and crafts and to help produce puppet shows. She held the job for two years while she lived at home once again, crowded as it was with Herman, Rose, and the three children. The job ended in 1938. Then, Pablita had a good offer that helped her make some money.

A famous man — who was a friend of the Indians and a founder of the Boy Scouts of America — lived in Santa Fe. His name was Ernest Thompson Seton. The Setons were planning a long trip through the eastern United States while Mr. Seton gave lectures. They needed someone to travel with them and take care of their baby. Knowing of Pablita's unusual talent, they decided to take her with them. It was her first trip away from her own state.

Seton had created a preserved area around his estate near Santa Fe where he could protect animals of many kinds from hunters. As he moved around the country, he told his audiences about the animal preserve. Seton was a popular lecturer. The Seton family and Pablita traveled from Nebraska, through New England, down the eastern seaboard, across to Arkansas, and along the southern route to New Mexico. They arrived back at Santa Fe in December, 1938.

Pablita was tired from the long trip. She had seen so many strange places, met so many new people, and eaten so much unusual food. She wanted to rest. She and Jane moved into Rosita's house while Rosita was away from the pueblo. Soon there were two changes in Pablita's life. Her younger sister Jane married and moved into her own house. Rosita came home, and there was not room for Pablita. This time, Pablita took a small room in the home of her uncle.

Pablita was twenty years old. Her sisters were now all married. Yet there was no one that Pablita wanted to marry. She loved her people, but somehow, coming home to the pueblo after her exciting trip was not altogether happy for her. There was something else she wanted to do. As she rested and helped her family with the chores, she dreamed of distant places.

One day in early 1939, a new challenge was offered to her. Olive Rush, the Santa Fe artist who had been such a good friend of the young people at the Indian School, asked Pablita if she would like to paint a mural. Olive Rush had been asked to supervise artists working on a painting in the open lobby of a new store in Albuquerque named Maisel's. The painting was to go all along the top part of a wall. It was up to Miss Rush to choose the artists to work with her. She remembered the work Pablita had done for the exhibit in Chicago. Miss Rush explained to Pablita that Maisel's sold only Indian crafts. They employed their own silver-smiths. They bought rugs and other items directly from the Indians. Out in front of their store they wanted good examples of Indian art. Pablita agreed to join the team. She went to Albuquerque and lived for several weeks with Herman's sister, Carmel, while working on the painting.

After Pablita and the other artists had done part of their murals, some vandals came at night and smeared them with cement. Pablita stayed in Albuquerque longer than she had expected and did her painting over. She painted a group of Santa Clara women standing in front of an adobe building. One of them carries her baby on her back. Each woman has a patterned shawl and straight, black hair.

In the front of the picture there is a row of large, black ollas. The sellers are waiting for their customers. In order to see Pablita's painting, a person must step in from the sidewalk. Then one can see the entire series of paintings that goes around the lobby. Each painting is signed by the artist.

Soon after the Maisel mural was finished, Pablita needed another job. Her skill at art came to her rescue again. Near the pueblo of Santa Clara there is a national park known as Bandelier National Monument. It is in Frijoles Canyon. The area was inhabited centuries ago by Cliff Dwellers. The remains of their houses are still standing high on the steep sides of the canyon. The Cliff Dwellers were farmers who planted their crops on the valley floor, yet lived high up on the canyon walls for protection. They carried all their supplies, including water, up the ladders. The ladders could be pulled up behind them.

The United States Park Service maintains a museum in

the park. In 1939, the supervisor was Dale King. Mr. King knew about Pablita Velarde's talent, and he needed paintings to go inside the glass cases of the museum. Behind displays of objects that had been found in the canyon, he wanted paintings to show how the Cliff Dwellers had lived. Mr. King asked Pablita to come out to the canyon and paint for the Park Service.

The young artist gladly accepted the job. She painted scenes from memories of her own childhood, because the life of the pueblos was much like that of the ancient peoples. The costumes, of course, were different. Modern Indians wear clothes made of cloth. The ancient people wore clothes of animal skins. Pablita painted pictures of drum making, herb gathering, and pottery making. She worked for nearly a year, painting the large panels. She made trips back to the pueblo occasionally. While at home, she talked to the old people, checking to be sure her paintings were correct. Sometimes the elderly Indians gave her good ideas to use in her art.

By 1940, the world war was beginning in Europe. The government needed money to train and expand our armed forces, which meant there was not much money for the Park Service. Mr. King had to let Pablita go in 1940.

After years of being crowded in someone else's house, Pablita decided to build one of her own. In 1939, she had begun building on a piece of land that her father gave her right next to his own. Pueblo women have been the builders for their people for centuries, but many of these traditional jobs for women are changing. Pablita did not build her home entirely alone. With money from her job at Bandelier National Monument, she hired a man to make adobe

Pablita's house at Santa Clara.

bricks. When they were ready, Herman picked them up in his wagon. Then he and his brother-in-law built a foundation with rocks and mud. On this they began building the adobe walls. They were building a three-room house. Nearly every house in the pueblo began with two or three rooms. As the years pass, if another room is needed, it is added to the original house. Jane's house now has eight rooms, although it began as only two.

Pablita kept paying for parts of her house with the money she was earning. After the walls were built, she had to pay for the vigas. These are stout, strong, young tree trunks laid on top the walls. The roof is built on top of them. The vigas show below the ceilings inside adobe houses, and they also stick out about one foot farther than the walls on the outside. Shadows from the beams slant down along the adobe walls all in a row.

Finally, after two years, Pablita's house had walls, a roof, and windows. It was time to plaster the inside and outside walls. Jane and her husband, Henry, came over to help. Henry made the adobe; Jane and Pablita plastered it over the bricks. Jane brought her new baby son with them. The sisters had fun together making a baby swing from an old buggy that had no wheels. This closeness of family members, each helping the other freely, is no longer true in the pueblo. Now, even in the family, money is expected for work. Only at big celebrations such as christenings, graduations, weddings, or funerals, does everyone help prepare for the gatherings.

By the summer of 1941, Pablita's house was ready. The walls were plastered inside and out. Inside, the walls were covered in new, bright whitewash. The windows and doors were painted. When Pablita moved in, her house was all paid for. Now she needed to furnish it. First, she bought a wood stove. She already had dishes, blankets, and a dinette table, but she needed a bed. She bought a bed and charged it. This was her first debt. It took courage to take on a debt, because earning money was not easy during those years, and Pablita knew she had to make the payments on time or else she would lose her bed. She was happy to be alone at last, not sharing crowded space with anyone. There was enough room for her to have her own studio. It was an unusual, brave idea for an Indian woman, living alone, to pay for and build her own home.

When her job in Bandelier National Monument ended, Pablita had to find another. The only thing she could find was a job in Española. She worked there in the back of an Indian trader's shop making drums. She decorated the drum tops. It was not a difficult job, but it was not a good job, either, and it did not pay well. During her free time, Pablita painted small paintings.

On the plaza in Santa Fe is one of the oldest buildings in the United States. It is known as the Palace of the Governors. The palace dates back to the time of the Spanish Conquest. It has a covered porch in front of it that provides a roof over the sidewalk along the entire city block. Indians display their handicrafts on the sidewalk. Pablita came in on weekends to display her paintings. Today, in Santa Fe, there are still Indians sitting in front of the palace with their silver jewelry, pottery, rugs, and Indian beads spread out on pieces of cloth. Tourists are happy to buy the Indian wares. Pablita made money selling her paintings. Those lucky tourists, who bought Pablita's small pictures at small prices, own work by an artist who is very famous now.

Pablita got along painting drums and small pictures, but she wanted a change with more promise of a better future. When the Bureau of Indian Affairs sent a supervisor to Santa Clara looking for high school graduates who needed jobs, Pablita went to see her. The supervisor offered Pablita a chance to become a trained switchboard operator in the telephone exchange at the large BIA office in Albuquerque. Pablita did not really want to be a telphone operator, but she wanted a better job and so she accepted the offer.

The BIA is the part of the United States Government that administers the affairs of American Indians. The Bureau is gradually turning over its power to Indians, but in 1941 the Bureau employees were very much in control. The office in Albuquerque is a central one that receives and sends many calls each day. Pablita, a successful artist, was not a successful telephone operator. She tried hard anyway, suffering from remarks about her mistakes. After the training ended, she became a regular operator.

Sometimes when another operator was sick and could not report to work Pablita would fill in for her. One evening, Pablita was filling in for an operator on the night shift. That evening, a young man came in to use the telephone. His name was Herbert Hardin. Herb worked as a night watchman at the BIA. It was the first time Pablita had seen him. He was friendly, laughing, and fun. Pablita was a fun loving girl. She was lonely in Albuquerque. She liked Herb and enjoyed his teasing. When Herb Hardin asked her for a date, she agreed to go out with him.

Pablita was a slender, bright-eyed, young woman with shiny, black hair and a pretty, wide smile. She liked to laugh and to talk with her friends, but in a group she was shy. She did not brag about her art. Herb liked her.

At twenty-three, Pablita was eight years older than her sister Legoria had been when she married. Pablita knew many young Indian men at Santa Clara. Most of them were in some way related to her family. Either they had relatives married to her relatives, or they were cousins. Pablita did not want to marry any of these men, or to live all her life in the pueblo. She had been away from the pueblo often; she had traveled around the United States, and she had grown used to living in an "Anglo" world. Anglo, in the Southwest, means non-Indian, or white man. Pablita liked living off the reservation where there were Anglos as well as Indians. She had never liked the idea that Indians should live only with Indians, away from the rest of society. Although she did not want to forget her proud Indian heritage, she wanted to be accepted as a person, rather than as an Indian.

At Santa Clara, the girls are free to choose their own husbands. They are not forced to marry a person chosen for them by a relative. The Indians do prefer that their daughters marry other Indians, either from Santa Clara or from another pueblo. Pablita did not follow this preference, just as she had not followed other accepted ways of the pueblo. She had not married young. She had not gone to the day school in the pueblo, but instead had gone all the way through high school in the city. She had built her own home. She had taken jobs that led to travel and living away from home. She had used her talent to develop a reputation as an artist, an occupation thought of as especially for a man. Pablita was an independent person by nature, and something of a rebel in her quiet way.

Herb Hardin courted Pablita for several months. He did not make a large salary, but he took Pablita to the movies and shared occasional meals with her. Mostly, they walked and talked. Soon Herb asked Pablita to marry him, and she accepted.

Pablita and Herb Hardin were married on Valentine's Day, 1942, at Santa Fe, in the rectory of the Cathedral of St. Francis. Herb and Pablita had no money for a honeymoon. They moved right into a small apartment in Albuquerque.

CHAPTER V

Winning
and Losing

Pablita Velarde was now Pablita Velarde Hardin, Indian wife of an Anglo man. She stayed on at the BIA as a telephone operator, working all day. Herb stayed on as night watchman, working all night. They lived on this schedule for two months, very happy in their own apartment. In April, Herb was drafted into the army and left for his basic training.

Later, Pablita and Herb lived for several months in Bastrop, a small town in Texas where Herb was stationed. They had a very bad house, with few conveniences and no telephone. Pablita was expecting her first baby, and she returned to Albuquerque while Herb went on to his next post. Pablita lived with Herb's relatives while she waited for their child to be born.

On May 28, 1943, Pablita gave birth to a beautiful baby girl. Her baby was given the Christian name, Helen. When Helen was one month old, Pablita took her to Santa Clara to live for a time. Qualupita came to perform the Indian naming ceremony, choosing a Tewa name that means "Blue Corn Tassles"; but Herman gave his granddaughter the name, "Little Standing Spruce," the same name as his beloved first wife, Marianita. This is the name by which Helen is known, and with which she signs her own works of art.

When Helen was five months old, Pablita and the baby crossed the United States to join Herb in Pennsylvania. The years 1941 to 1945 were war years, very unsettled for most everyone in the United States. They were hard years for the young Hardins. When Herb was ordered to California in 1944, he took Pablita back to Santa Clara to wait for their second child's birth, and he took Helen to stay with his parents in Clovis, New Mexico. Then Herb went on to the coast. A baby boy, named Herby for his father, was born in August, 1944. After he was one month old, Pablita went to Clovis to show Herby to his grandparents and to pick up Helen. All three returned to Santa Clara to wait for the end of the war. Pablita lived in the same house she had built before her marriage. She spent those years raising her children, making jewelry, painting, and creating small Indian dolls.

Herb got out of the army in 1945 and came home to Albuquerque to find a job. Although he could return to a night watchman job at the BIA — and did so for a while — Herb was eager to finish his college work. He hoped to join the police force, and for that he needed to be a college graduate.

Pablita helped Herb gain his goal. She moved to Richmond, California, so that she and the children could be with him while he attended the University of California in Berkeley. She continued to add to their income by painting. The Hardins lived on the GI bill, a government program for veterans that provides some money while the veteran goes to school. There was little money during those college years, but Pablita was used to a small income. She and Herb enjoyed their life in California for a time, but soon they found that Pablita could not remain there. Something about the air in the San Francisco Bay area was not good for Pablita. She had grown up on dry, clear desert air and became troubled by asthma in California. Herb realized that it was dangerous for her to stay there any longer. Once again, he had to be separated from his family. Pablita and the children went home to Santa Clara.

Helen was now three. Herby was two. Pablita was twenty-eight. She had been married for five years, and she was still waiting to have a home with her husband. Money was stretched very thin to cover both Herb's needs in California and the family's needs in Santa Clara, so Pablita decided she must continue to earn money herself.

Dale King was still director of the Bandelier National Monument. After the war ended, he had more funds to continue building the displays in the museum. He offered Pablita her old job back—if she could move out to Frijoles Canyon. Pablita accepted his offer quickly and happily.

This time, when she moved out to the canyon, she was not alone. Helen and Herby were with her. They lived in a cottage that was used in summer by the cowboys in the park. In winter, the park was closed to the public, so the cottage was available for the Hardins. Right beside it were the stables where all the park horses were penned at night. The park rangers were kind to the family — playing with the children, and watching them while Pablita painted. They chopped her wood and hauled it in for her stove. Helen and Herby had fun with the rangers' children. Sometimes they rode on a burro named Pasqualito. Squirrels came up to play with the children. At night, the deer came in from the woods and stole the food from the horses. In January, the snow fell so heavily that the canyon was snowbound all month; but in February, the canyon road was open when Herb came to spend his vacation with the family. Pablita continued on the job until late spring.

These paintings by Pablita Velarde in the Bandelier National Monument are among her finest works. They are the result of long hours of study and careful attention to detail. Students who study primitive cultures can learn many facts from Pablita's paintings. She realized the scientific importance of details and tried to be accurate about the style of headdress, moccasins, dresses, pottery design, and home designs.

At last, in June of 1947, Herb graduated with a bachelor's degree in criminology. From June until October, Herb searched for work. In October he joined the Albuquerque Police Department as a rookie, beginning a fine career in criminology. Herb was promoted steadily during his years on the force.

Pablita finally had a home with her husband and children. They lived at first in a rented house. It was hard to find new housing during the first few years after the war, but the Hardins did find a new home on a pleasant street during Herb's second year with the police department. This house has been Pablita's home in Albuquerque ever since.

As an artist, Pablita continued to improve. She entered her work in competitions throughout the western states, taking many prizes and getting much publicity in newspapers and magazines. The first important sale of her work was made in Tulsa, Oklahoma, to the Philbrook Art Center. She had sent paintings for many years to their annual In-

dian art show. Her first important prize was won there in
1948; winning it made Pablita feel she had really achieved
something and gave her confidence in her talent.

The Hardin home was nice, but it was small. There was
no special room for Pablita's studio, so she had to do her
painting in the kitchen. Pablita has a number of painting
techniques that call for equipment and space. She is especially famous for her earth paintings. To prepare for these, Pablita takes trips to many parts of the state collecting clays of

Pablita grinding earth colors.

various colors. She also gathers stones that she crushes in a metate with a mano. The metate is a shallow bowl carved of stone. The mano is a stone held in the hand. The artist pounds the colored rocks into powder and then sifts them, saving the colored powders and clays in jars. These are her pigments. She mixes these colors with glue and water and then paints with the mixture on pieces of masonite. After the paintings are completed, they must be framed. Pablita makes her own frames — sawing, gluing, nailing, and then painting them. Finally, she puts her paintings into the frames, nails them, adds wires so they can be hung, and puts clean backing on them. All these activities make things messy. Herb was irritated by the art materials in his home. He wanted Pablita to move all of them out to the garage, away from the house.

Pablita painted and also made Indian dolls and purses by hand which were sold at fairs and in shops. Each year, Pablita sent her paintings to the big art shows for Indian artists. Each year she won prizes, and her name was in the newspapers more frequently. People asked her to give talks about her art. She appeared on television explaining pueblo life. However, she spent most of her time at home caring for her family. Herb continued to do well on the police force, climbing rapidly to the rank of lieutenant. The Hardins did not go to parties or have a very active social life. They lived a quiet life.

In 1952, Dorothy Dunn wrote an article about Pablita and her art. It told about her life very briefly, and then mentioned that she lived in Albuquerque and was the wife of Herbert Hardin. Miss Dunn's article was published in *El Palacio*, the magazine of the Museum of New Mexico in

Pablita and Dorothy Dunn (on the right)
receiving Palmes' Academiques.

Santa Fe. Somehow this small magazine got to England where it was read by Mrs. Robert Aitken.

Mrs. Aitken sent Pablita a letter and a photograph. She told about visiting Santa Clara Pueblo in 1910. She said that Herman and Marianita had been kind to her during her stay. She had taken a picture of them together, and she wanted Pablita to have it. This mysterious and exciting letter brought a glow of pure joy into Pablita's life. She had never seen a photograph of her mother. The Indians were too poor to own cameras and take pictures when Herman was a young man. Pablita was so young when her mother died that she could not remember how she looked. In a way, the photograph from the English woman, so far away and from so long ago, restored Marianita to Pablita.

Recognition for her art brought Pablita several top honors. In 1954, with twelve others, Pablita was awarded a decoration from the French Government, known as the Palmes' Academiques. This award is given for an outstanding contribution to the field of art. Dorothy Dunn was another recipient; most of those awarded the decoration were pupils of Dorothy Dunn's in Santa Fe. This was the first time that Indian art was given recognition by a foreign government. The award was presented at a ceremony in Gallup, New Mexico. Herb and the children were there to watch Pablita receive it.

In 1955, Pablita took all the top prizes at the Inter-Tribal Indian Ceremonial in Gallup. She won the grand prize as well as first prizes in three other categories. Again, Herb and the children were there with her.

In 1956, Pablita painted a twenty-one foot mural for a restaurant in Houston, Texas. She did the work on masonite panels in her home in Albuquerque. Recreating a scene of the pueblo ceremonies, her mural is titled, "Green Corn Dance." Painting this mural was a hard, exhausting job. She worked very hard on it, finishing in six weeks. The mural was aggravating to Herb.

At first, Herb was proud of Pablita's success. He was grateful for her hard work through the years that had helped make it possible for him to finish his degree at the University of California. Yet, he did not really like the attention she was getting or the time Pablita spent on her art. Gradually, the home life of the Hardins became less happy. At times, Herb and Pablita were still close to each other. At other times there were long silences between them. During the middle of the 1950s, mostly because of the increasing unhappiness of her marriage, Pablita decided to renew her relationship with her own family at the pueblo.

Pablita remembered the tales her father told around the fire at night during her childhood. "Why," she wondered, "don't I write those stories down for others to enjoy?" She realized that she had forgotten a few parts of the stories, and she wanted to hear them all again. She began driving up to Santa Clara to visit with Herman.

Pablita's father was in his seventies. He and Pablita had lived separate lives for many years. Although Pablita loved her father and he loved her, they needed time to become close again. Pablita would find Herman out in front of his house sitting under the big cottonwood tree. After her long drive from Albuquerque, she would join Herman there, giving him a small gift of new socks or tobacco.

In the Tewa language her old father would say gruffly, "Sit down." Then he might not talk again for a long time.

Pablita might ask, "Are you hungry? Shall I fix you some-
thing to eat?" Herman would say, "If you want to." Slowly,
Pablita explained that she hoped to relearn all the wonder-
ful stories Herman had told the pueblo children long before.
She wanted to write them in English, and to illustrate them.
At first, Herman did not want to help her. He felt that the
stories were private, and only for the people of Santa Clara
to know. Pablita told him that there were not many Santa
Clarans who could carry on the tradition of storytelling.
She told him that the old ways of Santa Clara were fast dis-
appearing and that she wanted to help save the culture of
her people. With Herman's help, she could bring apprecia-
tion of the Indians' own heritage to those outside the pueblo. Herman became enthusiastic about this plan, and he
agreed to help her.

Herman asked her what she remembered about the story
of the stars. Pablita told him in Tewa. Then Herman told
her the story, explaining parts she might have forgotten. On
another visit they would go over another tale. Herman and
Pablita became close friends again by sharing these ancient
stories. Herman had not made up the stories; he had faith-
fully remembered them from his own childhood.

One of her first illustrations for Herman's stories was a
painting called "Old Father, The Story Teller." It was this
one that took the grand prize at the Inter-Tribal Indian
Ceremonial at Gallup in 1955.

Working on these stories helped Pablita during a very
difficult period in her life. She was deeply worried about
her marriage, which was becoming more and more un-
happy. Herb was interested in Pablita's work on the Indian
stories and occasionally helped her by improving the choice

of words she used in English, and by correcting her grammar. Then, without warning, he grew quite silent, losing interest in this and in Pablita's other projects; he was not happy. Finally, Herb decided to leave his home.

Because it was Christmas time and their father was gone, Pablita decided to take the children on a trip into Arizona to cheer them up. She drove west along Highway 66. In Globe, Arizona, they had car trouble, so Pablita took the car to a garage. On a hunch, while waiting for the car to be repaired, Pablita looked in the phone book to see if Dale King still lived in Globe. He had retired from the Park Service some years before; she had heard he was living in Globe. Pablita was delighted to find his name in the book, and she called him. Mr. King had not seen Pablita since that long winter in Bandelier National Monument. "Stay there," he said, "I will come in and pick you up. You must spend the night with us."

The Dale Kings and Pablita had a lot of catching up to do. He wanted to know what Pablita had been doing. She told him about the book of stories told by her Old Father. Dale King was very interested in Pablita's book. He told her that he had gone into the publishing business and might publish her book. When Pablita left Globe the next day, she had agreed to complete her stories and all the illustrations. Dale King told her he wanted to publish the book when it was ready. Their business venture was going to be a great success, but they did not know it then.

Pablita worked on the book, painting the illustrations and finishing the writing; it helped to take her mind off the breakup of her marriage. The Hardins were divorced in July, 1959. Her book, *Old Father, the Story Teller,* was published in 1960. The book received excellent reviews. It was selected as one of the best western books of the year. In 1961 it was chosen for a book exhibit held in Los Angeles. Pablita became widely known as an author as well as a painter. Other stories by her have been published in magazines but none of these exciting honors could erase the sadness she felt at the collapse of her marriage.

CHAPTER VI

Anglo and Pueblo

The first few years after the Hardin's divorce were the most difficult of Pablita Velarde's life. The Catholic faith prohibits remarriage. Pablita, a devout Catholic, realized that she would have to build a new life for herself and her children and that she would have to do it alone. Herb agreed to support the children. It was up to Pablita to support herself.

She grew extremely thin from hard work and unhappiness. Never a person to give up in the face of trouble, Pablita made plans and carried them out, forcing herself to do things she had not been able to do before.

Over the years many people had seen Pablita's paintings. Some of them had asked to buy work from her when she had none to sell. Before the divorce, Pablita had been adding to the family income, but she had not tried to live only by painting. Now she built up her supply of paintings so that she was prepared to sell to visitors. The artist wrote to people who had expressed interest in buying her work, inviting them to visit her when they passed through Albuquerque. In this way, she made some sales.

She painted constantly, creating a wide range of earth paintings, using the ancient methods of her people with the natural earth as her pigments. Pablita painted delightful pictures of animals — cheerful, happy views of the New Mexico roadrunner, soft-eyed deer, little birds, and energetic horses. She painted scenes of pueblo life, particularly the dancers in the ceremonial activities of the fiestas. Many of her designs were abstract, using old Indian patterns as part of the paintings. One of her most beautiful series shows the Christmas story. Indians on their horses portray the Three Wise Men, and an Indian mother with her baby and husband are Mary, Jesus, and Joseph. Another scene shows a pueblo with the night fires burning in the background announcing the good news of the birth of Christ.

To meet the public, Pablita needed to get over her shyness. She joined the Toastmistresses International, a group which helps a woman improve her ability to give speeches. Gradually, Pablita lost her stage fright. She was often asked to give talks; now she agreed to give many. Traveling with her children when school was out, she always appeared in traditional Indian clothes. Her lecture trips took her as far away as Florida.

At the time of the divorce, when the artist was most in need of help, she made two friends who have remained her steadfast supporters. After seeing Velarde paintings in many places, Margarete and Fred Chase, Albuquerque dealers in Indian art, asked if they could handle her work. The Chases wanted to arrange a gallery for her so that she would have a permanent place for her work to be seen and bought by the public. Such an offer was most welcome to Pablita. The Chases now feature Pablita's work, the pottery of Pablita's older sister Legoria, a master potter, and the work done by Helen Hardin, Pablita's lovely daughter.

Each year Pablita has taken her work to the major Indian art shows. Hardly a year has passed without a request for personal appearances, prize ribbons, and sales. The income from her art is what supports Pablita. With it, she has paid for her home and for the necessary family station wagon. In her trusty "jalopy," as she calls it, Pablita has traveled throughout the Southwestern states, carrying her paintings to exhibits, or collecting the stones and clays for her earth paintings.

In 1968, Pablita received one of her greatest honors. The Philbrook Art Center in Tulsa gave her a special award for

Casein water color: The Flight.

her outstanding contributions to Indian art in America. Few artists have received this award, known as the Waite-Phillips trophy. It is presented only once in an artist's lifetime. The artist was given an elaborate silver cup in honor of the award. From 1946 to 1968 Pablita won thirteen awards at the annual show in Tulsa.

One of her paintings was selected by President Johnson as a gift to the Prime Minister of Denmark. There are paintings by Velarde in the Department of the Interior Building in Washington, D. C., as well as in the American embassies in Ecuador and Spain. Museums in San Francisco, Tulsa, and Santa Fe own her work. Many people have Velarde paintings in their private collections. In addition to the gallery owned by her friends, Margarete and Fred Chase, other galleries in Arizona and New York City have carried Pablita's work.

The price of success for Pablita has been hard and endless work. To supply the paintings her galleries ask for, she must paint more than one hundred works a year, or at least one painting every few days. Because she is a serious artist, Pablita gives each painting a special meaning, relating it to her Indian past. She uses symbols and designs from the religion of the pueblo people, not just the people of Santa Clara. One of her most famous paintings is of a ceremony in Taos, the best-known pueblo along the Rio Grande River. To produce these works, she has become a student of Indian culture, using her art to interpret American Indian life.

Living as she has in the Anglo world, Pablita is able to see the changes in the pueblo clearly on her return visits. Even the buildings in the pueblo look different. The old two-story adobes are falling into ruin along the plaza. Young pueblo families are building modern houses at the edges of the area. Television dominates the pueblo home, as it does the Anglo one. Few children hear the tales that Old Father told when Pablita was a child. As a result, children are growing up knowing English better than they know Tewa. They know less of their own religious tribal beliefs than of the Christian faith; the pueblo has members of many churches now. The pickup truck has replaced the wagon as transportation. Jobs in the atomic city of Los Alamos up on the mountain have provided good incomes to the families of many Santa Clarans. The changes are helping the Indians become a part of the Anglo world, but they also mean the end of an ancient pattern of living.

In 1965, when the artist's son Herby was married to a beautiful girl from Germany, Pablita decided to let them live in her Albuquerque home while she returned to Santa Clara. For many years she had anticipated returning to her pueblo. She had exciting and important plans. Pablita wanted to record the legends, the religious beliefs, and the folk tales of her people in her native language. She bought one of the modern homes in Santa Clara; her own house that had served her well early in her life had been sold just after the divorce to raise needed cash. Pablita moved into her new house expecting to have more time to paint and to renew close friendships with her old pueblo neighbors.

At first, she spent many hours explaining her plan to the tribal officials. The Indians often do not want to set down the ancient beliefs of their people; they believe sacred things must be kept secret from the outside world. Pablita told them she wanted to save the sacred things for her own people, lest they be lost. At last, she started her work making tape recordings about the tribal culture. After some months of work, Pablita began to sense a hidden, unfriendly force directed against her. She describes it as the presence of "evil spirits" who were opposed to her revealing any more about her culture. All of the material she collected and recorded is in safekeeping; its whereabouts is a secret. Not sure whether the unfriendly feeling was from her ancestors or from the people of the pueblo itself, Pablita was saddened and left the pueblo after two years. She returned to Albuquerque and again took up her life among the friends she had made through the years.

Her weekly schedule still is one of day and night work. She paints during the day and builds frames at night. On Saturdays she cleans her house. On Sundays she goes to mass. Pablita's life is blessed with grandchildren. Helen has a girl Margarete; Herby has a son named Ralph William. Her children and grandchildren give her love and pleasure. They are a close family. The Hardins, relatives of Herb, are still a part of her life. The Velarde sisters, too, remain friends.

The Velarde talent has been inherited by Helen Hardin, who is becoming well-known for her own style of modern Indian art. Pablita and Herb Hardin have both helped Helen in her career. Herb Hardin has been with the State Department, living in various countries of South America for many years. He arranged a one-woman show for Helen when she visited him in Bogota, Columbia, for six months in 1968. She made many sales there. After she returned to the United States, she continued to paint, working on the same difficult schedule as her mother.

Pablita is a part of two worlds. Success and honor have come to her in the Anglo world. The pueblo points with pride to her in their published tourist guides, mentioning that Santa Clara is her birthplace. Nevertheless, painful experiences have come to her from the pueblo as well as from Anglo society. Pablita has not lost her old loyalties to her people or to the Catholic faith. Her art is still a mixture of both. Although her children are only one-half Indian and her grandchildren are only one-fourth Indian (both of her children married Anglos), Pablita has passed on her Indian heritage to her family. She continues to own land on the reservation, awaiting her possible return to Santa Clara to live, and perhaps to open her own gallery.

However, the Santa Clara Reservation is not the reservation she once knew. Now it has become a popular tourist camping ground, offering pine-sheltered campsites beside the rushing creek to many visitors through the spring, summer, and fall. The Puye Ruins, once scampered over by the Velarde girls, are now open to the public, with a gate house and guides. A paved highway links the pueblo and the reservation with the major roads throughout the state. The pueblo is not the friendly home of Pablita's childhood. She cannot forget the hostility she experienced in 1966. For all these reasons, Pablita must decide carefully what she wants to do in the future.

Pablita Velarde is today a beautiful Indian woman. Now in her fifties, she is the most famous Indian woman painter in the world. Recently, she and Helen and Margarete appeared as actresses on a major television program, a new experience and a pleasant one. She continues to try new things. Each honor and achievement has come to Pablita without spoiling the person she has always been. She is modest and friendly, and has a very funny sense of humor that brings a quick smile to her face. She wears her long, black hair with bangs, in the Indian fashion. Her eyes are a twinkling brown. The unhappiness she has known has not dampened her adventurous spirit, nor slowed down her art work. After many years of fame, but also much loneliness, Pablita Velarde is still Golden Dawn of Santa Clara Pueblo. She brings warmth and light into the lives of those around her, just as Qualupita prayed for at her birth.

THE AUTHOR

Mary Carroll Nelson has a bachelor's
degree from Barnard College in fine arts
and a master's degree in art education
from the University of New Mexico.
She has taught art to adults and children,
and is a professional artist. Mrs. Nelson
and Pablita Velarde are members of
the same branch of the National League
of American Pen Women in Albuquerque.

Designed by Tom Chambers

OTHER BIOGRAPHIES
IN THIS SERIES ARE

Joseph Brant
Geronimo
Chief Joseph
King Philip
Osceola
Powhatan
Red Cloud
Sequoya
Sitting Bull
Tecumseh
William Warren
William E. Beltz
Robert L. Bennett
LaDonna Harris
Oscar Howe
William W. Keeler
Maria Martinez
Billy Mills
Benjamin Reifel
Buffy Sainte-Marie
Maria Tallchief
James Thorpe
Annie Wauneka